# LETTER SOUNDS
# WORKBOOK

## LETTER SOUND CUT-AND-PASTES & COLORING ACTIVITIES

# SARAH FORST
## THE DESIGNER TEACHER

## Instructions for Use

The activities in this book are perfect for introducing and reinforcing letter sounds. It only features the primary sound for each letter to avoid confusion. For example, only the hard g sound is included (glove, game), and not soft g (germ, giraffe). If you or your little one are unsure of what any of the pictures represent, check the key on page 84.

The first three sections of the workbook are cut and paste activities that progress from easiest to hardest. The last section is a coloring page for each letter (except X, since it is not frequently used as a beginning letter). You may wish to have your child complete them in a different order– start with the letters your child knows best.

## Tools Needed

Name: _____ Date: _____

# Cut out the pictures and sort by sound.

| Mm | Ss |
|---|---|
| | |

Name: _____ Date: _____

# Cut out the pictures and sort by sound.

| Ff | Bb |
|----|----|
|    |    |

Name: _____ Date: _____

# Cut out the pictures and sort by sound.

| Aa | Rr |
|---|---|
| | |

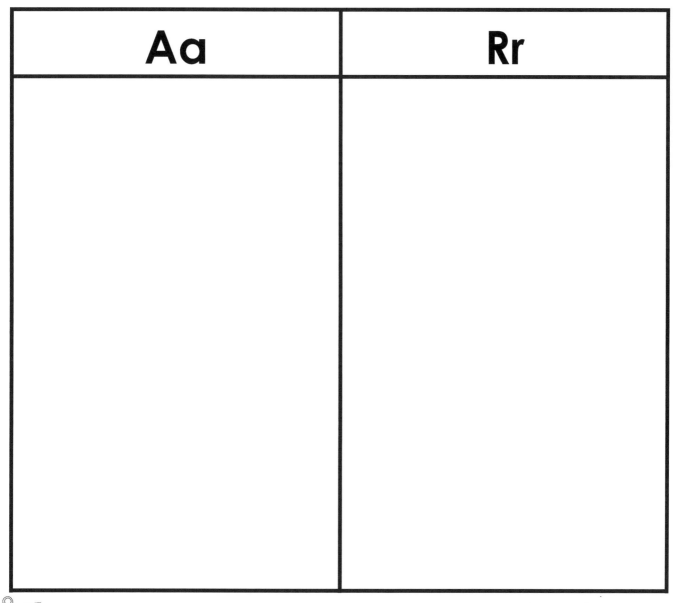

Name: _____ Date: _____

# Cut out the pictures and sort by sound.

| Tt | Cc |
|---|---|
|  |  |

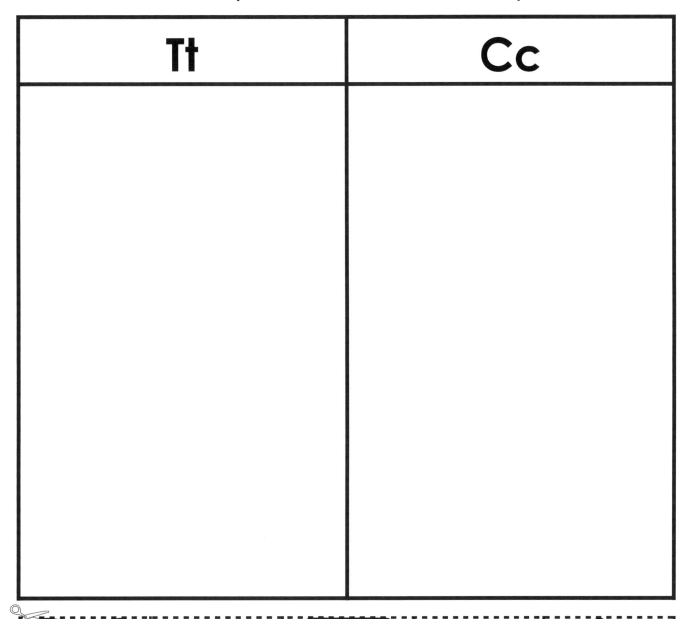

Name: _____ Date: _____

# Cut out the pictures and sort by sound.

| Pp | Ll |
|---|---|
|  |  |

Name: _____ Date: _____

# Cut out the pictures and sort by sound.

| Hh | Nn |
|---|---|
| | |

Name: _____ Date: _____

# Cut out the pictures and sort by sound.

| Ii | Dd |
|---|---|
|   |   |

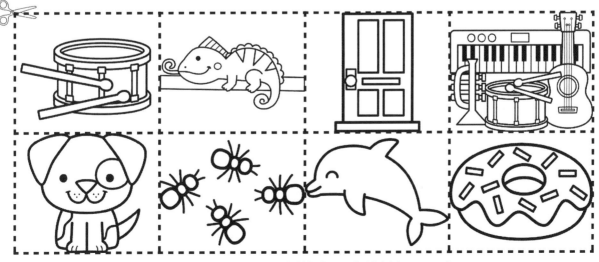

Name: _____ Date: _____

# Cut out the pictures and sort by sound.

| Oo | Gg |
|---|---|
|  |  |

Name: _____ Date: _____

# Cut out the pictures and sort by sound.

| Ee | Ww |
|---|---|

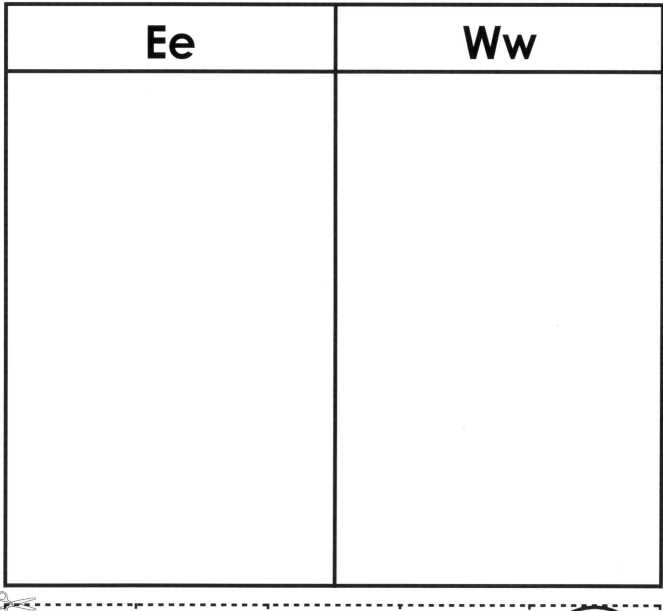

Name: _____ Date: _____

# Cut out the pictures and sort by sound.

| Jj | Vv |
|---|---|
| | |

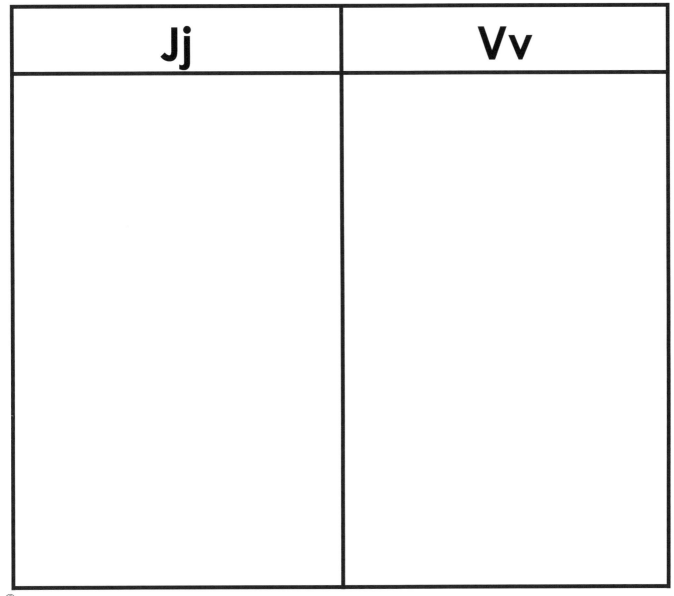

Name: _____ Date: _____

# Cut out the pictures and sort by sound.

| **Zz** | **Kk** |
|---|---|
|  |  |

Name: _____ Date: _____

# Cut out the pictures and sort by sound.

| Qq | Yy |
|---|---|
|  |  |

Name: _____ Date: _____

# Cut out the pictures and sort by sound.

| Uu | Bb |
|---|---|
|  |  |

Name: _____ Date: _____

## Cut out the pictures and sort by sound.

| Mm | Aa | Bb |
|---|---|---|
|  |  |  |

Name: _____ Date: _____

# Cut out the pictures and sort by sound.

| Ss | Tt | Rr |
|---|---|---|
|  |  |  |

Name: _____ Date: _____

## Cut out the pictures and sort by sound.

| Oo | Ww | Jj |
|---|---|---|
|  |  |  |

Name: _____ Date: _____

# Cut out the pictures and sort by sound.

| **Gg** | **Vv** | **Kk** |
|---|---|---|
| | | |

Name: _____ Date: _____

## Cut out the pictures and sort by sound.

| Ll | Nn | Ii |
|----|----|----|
|    |    |    |

Name: _____ Date: _____

## Cut out the pictures and sort by sound.

| **Hh** | **Dd** | **Ee** |
|--------|--------|--------|
|        |        |        |

Name: _____ Date: _____

# Cut out the pictures and sort by sound.

| Zz | Cc | Uu |
|---|---|---|
|  |  |  |

Name: _____ Date: _____

# Cut out the pictures and sort by sound.

| Ff | Yy | Pp |
|---|---|---|
|  |  |  |

Name: _____ Date: _____

# Cut out the pictures and match by sound.

| Mm | | | Ww | |
|----|---|---|----|---|

| Oo | | | Ss | |
|----|---|---|----|---|

| Aa | | | Tt | |
|----|---|---|----|---|

| Rr | | | Bb | |
|----|---|---|----|---|

# Cut out the pictures and match by sound.

| Jj | | Ll | |
|----|--|----|--|
| Vv | | Ii | |
| Kk | | Hh | |
| Nn | | Dd | |

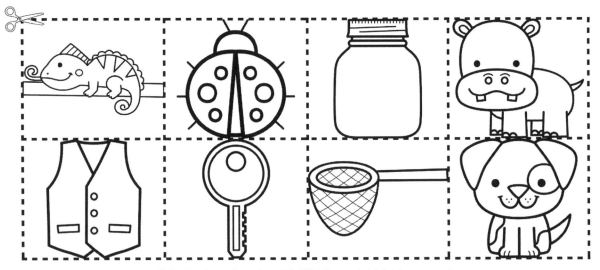

Name: _____ Date: _____

# Cut out the pictures and match by sound.

| | | | | |
|---|---|---|---|---|
| **Gg** | | **Ee** | |
| **Zz** | | **Cc** | |
| **Uu** | | **Ff** | |
| **Yy** | | **Pp** | |

Name: _____ Date: _____

# Cut out the pictures and match by sound.

| | | | |
|---|---|---|---|
| **Qq** | | **Ff** | |
| **Cc** | | **Hh** | |
| **Bb** | | **Ss** | |
| **Rr** | | **Aa** | |

# Cut out the pictures and match by sound.

| Pp | |
| Kk | |

| Ss | |
| Gg | |

| Tt | |
| Ll | |

| Rr | |
| Ff | |

Name: _____ Date: _____

# Cut out the pictures and match by sound.

| Yy | | Ww | |
|---|---|---|---|

| Pp | | Bb | |
|---|---|---|---|

| Dd | | Hh | |
|---|---|---|---|

| Ss | | Tt | |
|---|---|---|---|

Name: _____ Date: _____

## Color or circle the pictures that start with the letter.

Name: _____ Date: _____

## Color or circle the pictures that start with the letter.

**Bb**

Name: _____ Date: _____

## Color or circle the pictures that start with the letter.

Name: _____ Date: _____

## Color or circle the pictures that start with the letter.

**Dd**

Name: _____ Date: _____

## Color or circle the pictures that start with the letter.

**Ee**

Name: _____ Date: _____

## Color or circle the pictures that start with the letter.

Ff

Name: _____ Date: _____

# Color or circle the pictures that start with the letter.

**Gg**

Color or circle the pictures that start with the letter.

Name: _____ Date: _____

Color or circle the pictures that start with the letter.

**Ii**

Name: _____ Date: _____

## Color or circle the pictures that start with the letter.

Jj

**Name:** _____ **Date:** _____

# Color or circle the pictures that start with the letter.

## Kk

Color or circle the pictures that start with the letter.

**Ll**

Name: _____  Date: _____

## Color or circle the pictures that start with the letter.

**Mm**

Name: _____ Date: _____

# Color or circle the pictures that start with the letter.

**Nn**

Name: _____ Date: _____

# Color or circle the pictures that start with the letter.

Name: _____ Date: _____

Color or circle the pictures that start with the letter.

**Pp**

Name: _____ Date: _____

## Color or circle the pictures that start with the letter.

Qq

Name: _____ Date: _____

## Color or circle the pictures that start with the letter.

**Rr**

Name: _____ Date: _____

Color or circle the pictures that start with the letter.

**Ss**

Name: _____ Date: _____

## Color or circle the pictures that start with the letter.

**Tt**

Name: _____ Date: _____

## Color or circle the pictures that start with the letter.

Uu

Name: _____ Date: _____

## Color or circle the pictures that start with the letter.

Name: _____ Date: _____

## Color or circle the pictures that start with the letter.

**Ww**

Color or circle the pictures that start with the letter.

Name: _____ Date: _____

# Color or circle the pictures that start with the letter.

**Zz**

# Picture Key

| | |
|---|---|
| **A** | alligator, ant, astronaut, apple |
| **B** | bike, bat, bee, butterfly, banana, balloon, book, baby, bird |
| **C** | cat, cone, carrot, cloud, candle, cake, castle |
| **D** | drum, door, dog, dolphin, donut, deer, dress, dinosaur |
| **E** | elephant, egg, elf, elbow, elevator, envelope |
| **F** | fish, flamingo, flag, flower, frog, foot, fork, football, feather |
| **G** | glove, grass, ghost, glue, glasses, game |
| **H** | hammer, hippo, helicopter, hot dog, house, heart, helmet, horse, hand |
| **I** | iguana, instruments, insects |
| **J** | jar, jacket, jellyfish, juice, juggle |
| **K** | kangaroo, kitchen, kite, key, kiss, koala |
| **L** | ladybug, leaf, lion, lollipop, lamp, ladder, lobster |
| **M** | monkey, mushroom, mountains, mouse, milk, moon, mailbox, mittens |
| **N** | net, nose, needle, narwhal, nest |
| **O** | octopus, ostrich, oven, owl, otter |
| **P** | pineapple, pizza, penguin, pumpkin, pencil, pretzel, pie |
| **Q** | question, quilt, queen, quack |
| **R** | ring, rainbow, rake, raccoon, robot, rhino |
| **S** | scissors, spider, sock, snail, snake, spoon, sun, snowman, star |
| **T** | turtle, train, tent, tiger, tree, tractor, toothbrush |
| **U** | umbrella, up, underwear |
| **V** | vest, vegetables, volcano, vet, vacuum, van |
| **W** | wagon, watermelon, wheel, whale, web, watch |
| **Y** | yawn, yoga, yarn, yoyo, yolk, yak, yogurt |
| **Z** | zebra, zigzag, zipper, zoo |

For more learning resources, visit
**thedesignerteacher.com**

Made in the USA
Columbia, SC
10 February 2025

53649052R00048